For Stephen and Kristy—near to my heart though far away.

LARRY

✦

To my dear wife, Pat, who keeps me in the manner to which I have become accustomed.

DAVID

ACKNOWLEDGMENTS

I am indebted to Werner Franz for the gift that is his story; to my wife, Jo, who encouraged me to write it; to my editor, Amy Lennex, and the rest of the Sleeping Bear team for seeing promise in the idea; and to *Hindenburg* authority Patrick Russell for ensuring that the story was told correctly. Thank you each and every one.

LARRY

I wish to thank my friends Daniel Martin, who helped me bring Werner to life, and Aaron Novodvorsky, my ever-dependable research assistant.

Special thanks are due to Patrick Russell—his knowledge of the *Hindenburg* and her passengers was invaluable to me during the researching and painting for this book.

DAVID

Sleeping Bear Press™
315 E. Eisenhower Parkway, Suite 200
Ann Arbor, MI 48108
www.sleepingbearpress.com

Sleeping Bear Press is an imprint of Gale, a part of Cengage Learning.

10 9 8 7 6 5 4 3 2 1

Printed by China Translation & Printing Services Limited, Guangdong Province, China. 1st printing. 11/2011

Library of Congress Cataloging-in-Publication Data

Verstraete, Larry.
Surviving the Hindenburg / by Larry Verstraete ; illustrated by David Geister.
p. cm.
Summary: "Based on a true story, fourteen-year-old Werner Franz works as a cabin boy aboard the German zeppelin, the Hindenburg, and resourcefully survives its fatal crash"—Provided by publisher.

ISBN 978-1-58536-787-0

1. Hindenburg (Airship)—Juvenile literature. 2. Aircraft accidents—New Jersey—History—20th century—Juvenile literature. 3. Airships—Germany—History—20th century—Juvenile literature. 4. Franz, Werner, 1922-—Juvenile literature. 5. Cabin boys—Germany—Biography—Juvenile literature. 6. Aircraft accident victims—New Jersey—Biography—Juvenile literature. 7. Survival—New Jersey—History—20th century—Juvenile literature. I. Geister, David, ill. II. Title.
TL659.H5V47 2012
363.12'4—dc23   2011027879

Surviving the

HINDENBURG

Written by Larry Verstraete and Illustrated by David Geister

Long ago when air travel across the ocean was just beginning, mighty zeppelins ruled the skies. Zeppelins were giant airships. They had metal frames that were covered with fabric. Inside, between the framework, inflatable bags held lighter-than-air gases that gave the zeppelins lift. Engines attached to the outside of the hull pushed the airships forward. Zeppelins defied gravity, skimming beneath the clouds, floating on air much as a ship floats on water.

Of all the great zeppelins, the largest was the *Hindenburg*. Built in Friedrichshafen, Germany, and launched in 1936, the *Hindenburg* was 804 feet long, just slightly shorter than the *Titanic*. As tall as a 13-story building, the *Hindenburg* had two main living areas tucked within its cavernous interior—an upper deck for passengers and a lower deck that contained the crew's quarters and other passenger rooms. When its massive gas cells were filled with hydrogen, a highly flammable gas, the *Hindenburg* could transport an immense load using very little power.

The *Hindenburg* was the world's first flying hotel, a luxury aircraft built for long-distance travel across the ocean. With the *Hindenburg*, the future of air travel looked bright.

All that changed in a single day. On May 6, 1937, after crossing from Germany to the United States, the *Hindenburg* was destroyed by fire as it attempted a landing at the Lakehurst Naval Base in New Jersey.

Incredibly, of the 36 passengers and 61 crew members aboard that day, 62 people survived. This is the story of the youngest crew member, Werner Franz.

As the *Hindenburg*'s cabin boy, 14-year-old Werner had many chores to do for the officers and crew—setting tables, washing dishes, making beds, cleaning boots and uniforms. Much of the time, Werner worked and lived on the lower deck. He helped the cooks in the small kitchen, ate his meals in the crew mess, or dining room, and slept in a snug bed inside a tiny compartment with canvas walls that he shared with one of the stewards.

To reach other places inside the airship, Werner walked the keel gangway, a narrow wooden path that ran through the belly of the *Hindenburg* from the stern at the back to the bow at the front. Using the gangway, he sometimes visited the mechanics stationed in the outer side pods who manned the four roaring engines and the riggers who worked overhead, keeping a watchful eye on the gas cells and hydrogen. In the control car, the captain and officers piloted the *Hindenburg*, steering it into helpful air currents and past dangerous storms. Sometimes Werner visited them, too, and brought along coffee.

But of all the places on the *Hindenburg*, Werner's favorite was a small area in the bow. From a window, Werner looked down at the blue and choppy Atlantic Ocean and at sailboats rising and falling with the waves. Icebergs gleamed white in the sun. Sometimes, in stormy weather, Werner even saw lightning flash from cloud to cloud.

Werner went to this quiet place by himself. "I couldn't pull myself away from the window," Werner would say later. "I was sorry when I had to do some work."

On the morning of May 6, 1937, the third day of the *Hindenburg*'s flight, the scenery began to change. Instead of ocean, Werner saw the seashore of Nova Scotia, Canada. Then the eastern part of United States appeared.

Excitement swept the *Hindenburg*. Passengers huddled around the windows of the upper deck. The *Hindenburg*'s journey was coming to an end.

By mid-afternoon, the *Hindenburg* was over New York City. It circled above the busy streets of Manhattan, skimming over skyscrapers. Below, trolley cars clanged their bells. Taxi drivers honked a greeting. From the observation deck of the Empire State Building, curious tourists waved.

"We saw nothing but an ocean of buildings far and wide," Werner wrote in his journal afterward. "The sidewalks were swarming with people."

The *Hindenburg* was due to land at Lakehurst, New Jersey. But strong headwinds over the Atlantic had slowed the airship. By the time the *Hindenburg* neared the airfield at four o'clock, it was already almost 12 hours late.

Time was a precious thing, especially for Werner, especially that day.

The *Hindenburg* was scheduled to return to Frankfurt, Germany, later that evening. Because it was Werner's first visit to the United States, he had dreamed of visiting New York City in the few hours between arrival and departure. But now...

A storm was brewing. Landing the *Hindenburg* in such conditions was risky. The captain gave the order to continue flying. They would return later. It would be safer that way. The *Hindenburg* flew southeast and then turned north, skirting along the beaches of New Jersey, giving passengers spectacular views.

By evening, the skies began to clear. Around seven o'clock, the *Hindenburg* returned to Lakehurst. It looped over the airfield, sweeping lower as it neared the mooring mast, its docking station.

While Werner put dishes away in the kitchen, more than two hundred men in the docking crew swarmed the airfield, ready to grab the mooring lines that would be dropped from the *Hindenburg*'s bow.

The *Hindenburg*'s first landing of the season was big news. Photographers and newsreel reporters readied their cameras. Spectators gawked and pointed. A mighty shout rose from the ground.

"There she is!"

In the officer's mess, Werner heard an announcement.

"Six men forward."

The stern was heavier than the bow. Before the mooring lines could be lowered, the zeppelin had to be leveled. To add extra weight to the bow, the captain ordered six crewmen to the front.

More than anything, Werner wished he could be one. The bow offered the best views of the landing. But Werner still had dishes to put away. He couldn't leave until he was finished.

Werner had a coffee cup in his hand when he heard a muffled thud. He felt the *Hindenburg* quiver, and saw a glow through the window. Without warning, the stern dropped. Dishes tumbled from the cabinet.

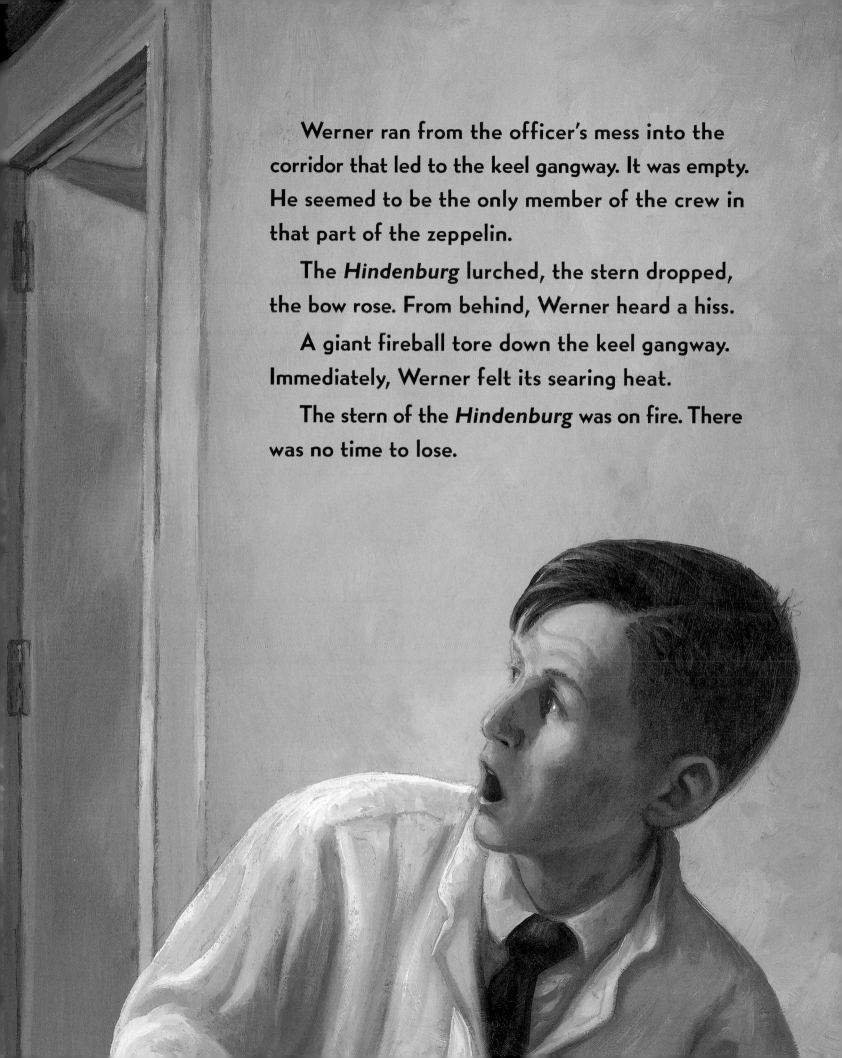

Werner ran from the officer's mess into the corridor that led to the keel gangway. It was empty. He seemed to be the only member of the crew in that part of the zeppelin.

The *Hindenburg* lurched, the stern dropped, the bow rose. From behind, Werner heard a hiss.

A giant fireball tore down the keel gangway. Immediately, Werner felt its searing heat.

The stern of the *Hindenburg* was on fire. There was no time to lose.

Werner ran toward the bow, but he managed only a few steps. He slipped and landed on his stomach. Backward, toward the fire, he slid.

Fighting the steep slope, Werner grabbed ropes on either side of the gangway and crawled. A roar filled his ears. Fed by exploding gas cells, flames shot forward, leaping across the fabric, surging ahead. In no time, the fire had spread from the stern, then to the midsection, now to the bow.

Heat scorched the soles of Werner's shoes. There didn't seem to be anywhere to go, no place safe, no easy escape.

Suddenly, a cold burst of water soaked Werner. A water tank had ruptured. The water drenched his clothes and protected him from the fire. For a moment, it quenched the terrible heat.

The cold shock sharpened Werner's senses, too. Somewhere in the smoke and haze, there had to be a way out.

Werner knew of one place—a hatch, a small opening, that led outside. He had used it to bring supplies aboard the *Hindenburg*.

It was getting harder to breathe. The flames were gaining speed. The *Hindenburg* was breaking apart.

Through the smoke, Werner saw the shadowy outline of the hatch. Using both feet, he kicked the hatch door open with all his might. Below, Werner saw the sandy soil of the airfield. He waited. One second. Two.

The *Hindenburg*'s stern had crumpled to the ground. Werner waited until the bow dipped and followed. Then he jumped.

The soft sand of the airfield cushioned Werner's fall, but for a moment he was too stunned to move.

"My mind didn't start working again until I was on the ground," Werner said later. "Then I started running."

When Werner was a safe distance away, he stopped. He stood and stared at the scene.

There were people everywhere. Their faces were blackened with soot. Their clothes were burned and tattered. Werner realized that these were passengers and crew from the *Hindenburg*. Like him, they had been lucky to escape.

But Werner also knew that not everyone had been so fortunate.

"After a while, it came to me," he said. "I lost my nerve. I cried and wailed like a baby. I didn't know what to do."

Some men approached Werner. They thought he was a visitor, there to watch the landing.

"They shook me to my senses," Werner said. "'*Get a hold of yourself and try to help someone*,' they told me. But there was no one left to help."

In German, Werner tried to tell them who he was. "Ich bin der cabin-boy vom *Hindenburg*!" he said over and over.

Finally, one of the men realized what Werner was saying. "Hey, this is the airship's cabin boy," he told the others.

Werner was taken to a hangar, where he was given dry clothes and warm food. Other survivors joined him. Together they sat in quiet shock, trying to understand what had just happened.

Later the group visited a nearby hospital to check on the more seriously injured survivors. Some were badly burned, and Werner knew they might never make it through the night.

Finally, Werner was taken to the airfield barracks. Exhausted, he fell asleep.

The next morning, Werner received permission to visit the wreck site. There was something he wanted, something he hoped to find.

The *Hindenburg* was barely recognizable. Little was left that could be identified: girders mangled and charred, windows melted and fused together, blackened serving dishes and cutlery scattered, and a singed mailbag stuffed with postcards and letters from Germany.

Werner walked around the wreck. There he found it. His pocket watch, the one given to him by his grandfather.

Like Werner, it had survived the *Hindenburg*.

After the
HINDENBURG DISASTER

Werner Franz

News of the *Hindenburg* disaster quickly traveled to Germany. In the confusion, Werner was mistakenly listed as one of the dead or missing. Within an hour, the report was corrected, but for a short time his parents believed he was one of the airship's casualties.

In the days afterward, Werner lived with the family of Anton Heinen, a former zeppelin test pilot who now worked for the U.S. Navy. After an inquiry into the disaster, Werner returned to Germany. Following World War II, he became a precision instrument maker. In the years that followed, he was often interviewed about his *Hindenburg* experience, and on several occasions he revisited the Lakehurst site.

Currently, Werner Franz lives in Bad Soden, Germany. He is the last surviving member of the *Hindenburg* crew. To this day, he credits his fortunate escape to the burst of water that soaked his clothes and enabled him to flee "wet—but alive."

The *Hindenburg* Inquiry

After the disaster, theories circulated about the fire's cause. Some suspected sabotage, others a lightning strike or electrical spark. An investigation was launched. Both the German and American governments inspected the wreckage, and witnesses were called to testify.

Investigators concluded that the explosion was caused by hydrogen leaking from a gas cell in the stern, possibly the result of a rigging wire that suddenly snapped and pierced the fabric. Static electricity, perhaps from the passing storm, ignited the escaping hydrogen. Fire spread quickly, and in 34 seconds, the *Hindenburg* was little more than charred and twisted rubble.

Recently, Addison Bain, a NASA scientist, proposed a different version of events: that the *Hindenburg*'s chemically treated fabric covering might have contributed to the fire. Bain conducted tests on fabric that had been treated with the same chemicals used on the *Hindenburg* and found that it became highly flammable. Although his theory is controversial and has been contested by some scientists, Bain believes that the fire began when a random spark ignited the fabric covering.

Regardless of the fire's origin, the *Hindenburg* disaster changed the course of aviation. People became distrustful of all forms of zeppelin travel, and remaining zeppelins were dismantled. Newly engineered airplanes rose to take their place. Faster and more efficient, the airplane also seemed to be a safer way to cross the ocean.

Other Survivor Stories

The chance of survival depended very much on where the passengers and crew were at the time. Because the fire started in the **stern**—the section that hit the ground first—and then raced forward, the crew stationed in the tail fared better than those in the bow. Mechanic Richard Kollmer was the first to escape. When the stern struck the ground, he escaped through an access hatch near one of the fins and ran.

As the fire leaped to other gas bags, confusion swept the **upper deck**. Passenger Leonhard Adelt said that the impact "threw us from the window to the stair corridor. The tables and chairs of the reading room … jammed us like a barricade." Adelt and his wife survived by dropping to the ground from a window just as the airship was about to hit the airfield.

Wilhelm Balla, one of the stewards, was in the **lounge** when the fire started. After helping passengers, once the bow dipped, he too jumped from a promenade window. Balla survived with only a twisted ankle.

There was a delay of a few seconds before the crew in the **control car** understood what was happening. As the stern dropped, the bow rose and officer Albert Sammt leaned out to look behind. "The ship's on fire!" he cried. Amazingly, all but one of those in the control car escaped the burning wreck.

Some were saved in freakish ways. Mechanic Theodor Ritter was in one of the **engine pods**, tight and very noisy spaces on the outside of the airship. At first, Ritter was unaware that there was a problem. He saw a flash of flame, but before he could react, the explosion ripped the engine pod loose. It landed in sand, crushed and mangled. Upon impact, Ritter was thrown out the back of the pod, suffering serious burns and injuries that required hospitalization.

Flames rushed through the center of the ship and exploded through the nose, turning the **bow** into a hydrogen-fed torch. Cook Alfred Grözinger was there and later said the ship "seemed to rise into the air. I planned to hold on to the frame until the ship hit the ground and then jump." Grözinger's plan worked. As the bow crashed to the ground, he let go and landed on his feet in the sand.

Hindenburg Memories and Memorials

Although the *Hindenburg* is no more, in a number of ways the memory of the great airship has been preserved:

Herbert Morrison Broadcast

Radio broadcaster Herbert Morrison was at the airfield to cover the *Hindenburg*'s first flight of the season. As flames consumed the airship, he was overcome with emotion. He continued the broadcast anyway, his words a jumble of haunting and terrifying impressions. "It's burst into flames! Get out of the way, please, oh my, this is terrible! It is burning, bursting into flames. Oh, the humanity and all the passengers!" Morrison's dramatic broadcast, synchronized to movie footage of the *Hindenburg* disaster, can be viewed on YouTube.

Lakehurst Naval Base—Lakehurst, New Jersey

The exact spot on the airfield where the *Hindenburg* crashed is marked with a memorial. Also at the Lakehurst site is a small museum containing a replica of the control car and artifacts salvaged from the wreck, as well as Hangar 1, the giant structure where the *Hindenburg* was sometimes stored.

Zeppelin Museum—Friedrichshafen, Germany

At the Zeppelin Museum, visitors can walk through fully equipped replicas of the *Hindenburg*'s promenade, lounge, reading room, smoking room, and passenger cabin. On display is a mock-up of the airship's girder-and-brace construction as well as artifacts salvaged from the *Hindenburg*.